SONGS FOR THE CHURCH
2023

50 SONGS FOR THE LOCAL CHURCH

Copyright Notice

No part of this publication may be reproduced in any form without the permission of the copyright holder of the songs and the publisher of the songbook. Exceptions to this rule are made for holders of licences issued by Christian Copyright Licensing International (CCLI), as follows:

CHURCH COPYRIGHT LICENCE
Churches and organisations holding a CCLI Church Copyright Licence may store and reproduce the lyrics of the songs for projection or print within the terms of their licence.

Licence holders may also make customised musical arrangements for transposing instruments such as wind and brass provided the melody line remains unchanged. This licence also permits translations of the lyrics into languages where no published version exists.

STREAMING/STREAMING PLUS LICENCE
Churches and organisations holding a CCLI Streaming Licence may stream or upload authorised songs within the terms of their licence.

CCLI's Streaming/Streaming Plus Licences are available as a supplement to the Church Copyright Licence.

MUSIC REPRODUCTION LICENCE
Churches and organisations holding a Music Reproduction Licence may photocopy, scan, and file-share the lyrics and/or music of the songs directly from this publication within the terms of their licence.

The Music Reproduction Licence is available as a supplement to the Church Copyright Licence.

UNAUTHORISED PHOTOCOPYING IS ILLEGAL and detrimental to the work and ministry of the songwriters and publishers.

All rights reserved. All songs are reproduced by kind permission of the copyright holders – names of which are shown below each song/hymn. Any omission of acknowledgement to a composer or publisher will be corrected in future editions. For further information about copyright licensing in the UK and Ireland please contact:

Christian Copyright Licensing International (CCLI)
Unit 16-17, Pacific House, 1 Easter Island Place, Eastbourne BN23 6FA
Tel: +44 (0)1323 436100
Email: uk@ccli.com
ccli.com

Acknowledgements

Artwork: Ascent Creative
Executive Producer: Phil Loose

Published & distributed by Essential Christian
14 Horsted Square, Uckfield, East Sussex, TN22 1QG, UK
Registered Charity number 1126997.

ISBN 978-1-911237-17-4

SONGS FOR THE CHURCH 2023

At Spring Harvest we have provided worship resources for the local church for over 40 years, and this year we are delighted to continue this with our latest songbook. Songs for the Church is a brand new songs resource for 2023 in partnership with our friends at CCLI, who share our heart to serve the Church.

In the following pages you will find songs from established writers as well as some new songwriters who are helping aid our worship with wonderful new songs. All of these people feel called to write for the local church and we hope that this songbook becomes a well-used resource in whatever context you lead worship.

We are aware that in an increasingly digital world many people find their song resources online so every chart in this book exists as a hybrid chord chart. As well as the lyrics and chords you see in the book, you'll notice that each song has a QR code alongside it. Scan this and it will take you to CCLI's SongSelect website where you will find sheet music and further song resources.

There are 50 songs in total including 10 All-Age songs where the whole church family can join in. Our hope and prayer is that this songbook is a helpful resource for you and we are delighted to be able to give it away for free this year and thankful for the support of global publishers to enable this.

If you are a worship leader or church musician we would love to let you know more about future resources from Songs for the Church and CCLI.

Sign up at **www.songsforthechurch.co.uk** to be the first to find out.

Song Index

1	A Thousand Hallelujahs
2	All Hail King Jesus
3	All You Do
4	Amen
5	Back To Life
6	By The Grace Of God
7	Church Unleashed
8	Fall On Us
9	God Of The Ages
10	Goodness Of God
11	Gratitude
12	Greater Than It All (It Is Finished)
13	He's Alive
14	Holy Forever
15	Honesty
16	Hymn Of The Saviour
17	I Speak Jesus
18	Justice
19	Kingdom Come (Lift Up Your Heads)
20	Lean In
21	Let Everything That Has Breath Praise
22	Lord We Pray For Peace
23	Love Around
24	Love Won't Stop
25	Make Room
26	Maker Of The Moon
27	More Than Enough
28	One People
29	Prayer Of Consecration
30	Pull Me Through
31	Raised With Christ
32	Same God
33	Son Of Suffering
34	Thank You
35	We Say Yes
36	What A Friend We Have In Jesus
37	You Are My Father (Child Of God)
38	You Are The Christ
39	You're Still God
40	You Restore My Soul

1 A THOUSAND HALLELUJAHS

Brooke Ligertwood, Phil Wickham, Scott Ligertwood
Suggested Key: D
BPM: 71 (4/4)

Verse 1
```
D                  G              D
  Who else would rocks cry out to worship
D                  G              D
  Whose glory taught the stars to shine
G         A             Bm7     A      G
  Perhaps cre - a - tion longs to have the words to sing
G         A      D
But this joy is mine
```

Chorus
```
G                  D
  With a thousand hallelujahs
A      Bm         A
  We magnify Your Name
G               D
  You alone deserve the glory
A        Bm       A
  The honour and the praise
G           A            D    D/F#  Bm   A
  Lord Jesus  this song is for - ev - er   Yours
       G         D/F#        A      D
A thousand hallelujahs and a thousand more
```

Verse 2
```
D/F#            G         D
  Who else would die for our redemption
D/F#              G         D
  Whose resurrection means I'll rise
G          A             Bm      A       G
  There isn't time enough to sing of all You've done
G        A         D
But I have eternity to try
```

Instrumental
D / / / | Em7 / / / | D/F# / / / | G / Asus A

Bridge
```
D             Em         D/F#
Praise to the Lord, to the Lamb
           G      Asus A
To the King of hea - ven
D             Em         D/F#
Praise for He rose, now He reigns
           G       Asus A
We will sing for - ev - er

Bm        A/C#         D
Praise to the Lord, to the Lamb
           G      Asus A
To the King of hea - ven
Bm        A/C#         D
Praise for He rose, now He reigns
D/F#       G        A
  We will sing for - ev - er
```

Brooke Ligertwood, Phil Wickham, Scott Ligertwood
© 2022 Phil Wickham Music / Simply Global Songs (Admin. by Small Stone Media BV, Holland (Admin. in the UK/Eire by Song Solutions www.songsolutions.org). City and Vine Music Publishing International (Admin. by IO Music Publishing UK).

CCLI #: 7190270

Further resources for this song are available at ccli.com/songbook

ALL HAIL KING JESUS

Jeremy Riddle, Steffany Gretzinger, Peter Mattis, Ran Jackson
Suggested Key: A
BPM: 75 (4/4)

Verse 1
A
There was a moment when the lights went out
F#m
When death had claimed its victory
E
The King of Love had given up His life
D
The darkest day in history

Verse 2
There on a cross they made for sinners
For every curse His blood atoned
One final breath and it was finished
But not the end we could have known

Pre-Chorus 1
      Bm F#m   E
For the earth began to shake
   A C#m7 D
And the veil was torn
     Bm F#m   E
What sacrifice was made
  A C#m7 D
As the heavens roared

Chorus
A   Asus4
All hail King Jesus
A   Asus4   C#m7
All hail the Lord of Heaven and earth
F#m7   D
All hail King Jesus
A/C#   E   A
All hail the Saviour of the world

Verse 2
There was a moment when the sky lit up
A flash of light breaking through
When all was lost He crossed eternity
The King of life was on the move

Pre-Chorus 2
For in a dark, cold tomb
Where our Lord was laid
One miraculous breath
And we're forever changed

Bridge
    E   F#m7   D   A   A/C#
Let every knee, come bow before the King of Kings
    E   F#m7   D   A   A/C#
Let every tongue, confess that He is Lord
    E   F#m7   D   A
Lift up your shout, let us join with all of Heaven
         E   F#m7   D   A
Singing Holy,
        E   F#m7   D   A
Singing Holy
        E   F#m7   D   A
Cry out Holy,
        E   F#m7   D
Cry out Holy

Jeremy Riddle, Steffany Gretzinger, Peter Mattis, Ran Jackson
© 2017 Richmond Park Publishing (Admin. by Essential Music Publishing LLC).
Bethel Music Publishing / Jeremy Riddle Music Designee (Admin. by Song Solutions).

CCLI #: 7097216

Further resources for this song are available at ccli.com/songbook

3 ALL YOU DO

Caz Talbot, Tom Smith
Suggested Key: F# (D Capo 4)
BPM: 174 (6/8)

Verse 1
D   A   Bm
You were there at the start,
                G
Creation's first breath
D   A   Bm   G
Held it all in Your hands, as You intended
D   A   Bm   G
The beauty of heaven and earth and the in-between
D   A   Bm   G
All as one bowing to The King of Glory

Verse 2
Bm   A
There never will, there'll never be
G   A
Anyone just like You Lord
Bm   A
There never will, there'll never be
G
Anyone just like You

Chorus 1
D
Great are You Lord in all you do
With my life I worship You
D
The highest of praises to You Lord
God You're worthy of it all

Verse 2
You were there on a cross
As You breathed your last breath
Laid inside a dark cold tomb. as You met with death
But You waged war in the depths of hell
Where You claimed your vict'ry
And in three days You rose to life
Jesus King of glory

Chorus 2
D   A   G
Great are You Lord in all you do
G
With my life I worship You
D   A   G
The highest of praises to You Lord
G
God You're worthy of it all

Instrumental
D   A   G

Bridge
Bm7   A G   A
Holy, Holy is the Lord almighty
Bm7   A   G
Worthy, worthy is Your name

Caz Talbot, Tom Smith
© 2021 Wings Music Group (Admin. by Sentric Music). Remaining portion is unaffiliated.

CCLI #: 7215067

AMEN ⬥4

Anna Hamilton and Grace Ibbott
Suggested Key: D
BPM: 69 (4/4)

Verse 1
```
        G          D/F#
We've built kingdoms in our names
         Bm          A
We've been distant, walked our own way
        G          D/F#
Seeking idols and not your face
                  Bm          A
But Father you're too precious to us to trade away
```

Chorus
```
       D           F#m7
So we come again, kneel at Your feet again
        G         G    A
And we say amen, let your will be done in us
```

Verse 2
We've seen injustice and let it be
Drawn our own lines on your masterpiece
With repentance, in humility
Father form in us the church You long to see

Bridge
```
         G             A
With no questions, no reservations
             D/F#               Bm7
Here we are, King of love, you have our hearts
             G            A
Let justice roll like a mighty river
             D/F#           Bm7
On and on, as we pray, your kingdom come
```

Anna Hamilton and Grace Ibbott
© 2022 Bespoke Records

CCLI #: 7200785

Further resources for this song are available at
ccli.com/songbook

5 BACK TO LIFE

Ben Fielding, Brian Johnson, Chris Davenport, Phil Wickham, Reuben Morgan & Zahriya Zachary
Suggested Key: B
BPM: 72.5 (4/4)

Chorus
```
          E      B      F#       G#m
No longer I who live but Christ in me
              E      B      F#     G#m
For I've been born again, my heart is free
                E          B        F#      G#m
The hope of heaven before me, the grave behind
        E           F#              B
Hallelujah, You've brought me back to life
```

Verse 1
B
I won't forget the moment

I heard You call my name
F#
Out of the grip of darkness, into the light of grace
E   B
  Just like Lazarus, You brought me back to life

Verse 2
Where there was dead religion
Now there is living faith
All of my hope and freedom
Are found in Jesus' name
Just like Lazarus, You brought me back to life

Verse 3
When something says I am guilty
I'll point to the price You paid
When something says I'm not worthy
I'll point to that empty grave
Just like Lazarus, You brought me back to life

Verse 4
How can I begin to thank You
For all that You've done for me
Jesus to fully praise You, it will take all eternity
Just like Lazarus, You've brought me back to life

Bridge
B
 The enemy thought he had me
          Bsus
But Jesus said 'You are mine'

B
 The enemy thought he had me
          G#m   E (F# back into chorus)
But Jesus said 'You are mine'

Ben Fielding, Brian Johnson, Chris Davenport, Phil Wickham, Reuben Morgan & Zahriya Zachary
© 2021 Phil Wickham Music/Simply Global Songs (Admin. by Small Stone Media BV, Holland (Admin. in the UK/Eire by Song Solutions www.songsolutions.org) ; Cdavs Music/Songs for TIM (Admin. by Capitol CMG Publishing) ; SHOUT! Music Publishing Australia (Admin. by SHOUT! Music Publishing UK) ; Bethel Music Publishing/Brian and Jenn Publishing/Zahriya Zachary (Admin. by Song Solutions)

CCLI #: 7183538

Further resources for
this song are available at
ccli.com/songbook

BY THE GRACE OF GOD

6

Brian Johnson, Kristene DiMarco, Tim Hughes, Nick Herbert and Martin Smith
Suggested Key: D
BPM: 72 (4/4)

Verse 1
```
   D     Dmaj7/F#  G   D
I rest my soul on    Jesus,
Bm7    Dmaj7/F#    G(2)
when the mountains shake
   D    Dmaj7/F#   G    D
I put my trust in    Jesus
      G    A    D         Dsus  D
The moment I awake
```

Verse 2
```
   D    Dmaj7/F#   G    D
And when my soul is lost at sea
Bm7    Dmaj7/F#   G(2)
He  will  be   my rock
     D    Dmaj7/F#   G    D
My vision be in   Christ alone,
       G       A        D
this grace is all we've got
```

Chorus
```
      G                 D
His love is like the mighty ocean
      G              Asus    A
His love for me will never stop
       Bm7              Dmaj7/F#   G
Oh His arms are strong enough to  carry  me
           D        A         D
Through it all by the grace of God
```

Verse 3
High upon His shoulders
Safely brought this far
Helper of my helpless soul
The king of broken hearts

Bridge
```
     G            A           Bm       Dmaj7/F#
You are the passion of my life, Lord Jesus
     G            A           Bm       Dmaj9/F#
You are the song within my soul
              G        A        Bm7      Dmaj7/F#
My strength, my hope,  my all   in    all
       G   Bm7         A
Is You,    Jesus You
```

Verse 4
When breath grows still and night draws near
I will not be afraid
I know the plans He has for me
Don't finish at my grave

Chorus 2
```
      G                 D
Your love is like the mighty ocean
      G              Asus    A
Your love for me will never stop
       Bm7              Dmaj7/F#   G
Oh your arms are strong enough to carry me
           D        A         D
Through it all by the grace of God
```

Brian Johnson, Kristene DiMarco, Tim Hughes, Nick Herbert and Martin Smith
© 2019 Capitol CMG Genesis/Safe & Sound Music (Admin. by Capitol CMG Publishing) ; Thankyou Music/Tim Hughes Designee (Admin. by Integrity Music Ltd) ; Bethel Music Publishing (Admin. by Song Solutions)
Remaining portion is unaffiliated

CCLI #: 7143863

Further resources for this song are available at
ccli.com/songbook

7 CHURCH UNLEASHED

Will Johnson and Mim Johnson
Suggested Key: G
BPM: 110 (4/4)

Chorus
```
                       G
We're not people of fear
                 C
We are people of courage
                    G/B
We're not people of greed
                C
But of generous heart
                    Em7
We're your people O God
                    C
We are giving and loving
                  Em7          D
So wherever we are whatever it cost
                  G/B                    C
For as long as it takes we will follow your call
                    G      Am7    C
Let your church be unleashed
                    G      Am7    C
Let your church be unleashed
```

Verse
We're not people of fear
But we're people of courage
We're not people of greed
But of generous heart
We're your people O God
We are giving and loving
So wherever we are whatever it cost
The world it might be in lockdown
But We'll follow your call
Let your church be unleashed
Let your church be unleashed
Let your church be unleashed
Let your church be unleashed

Will Johnson and Mim Johnson
© 2020 Song Solutions Daybreak (Admin. By Song Solutions www.songsolutions.org)

CCLI #: 7150098

Further resources for this song are available at
ccli.com/songbook

FALL ON US

8

Damares Gomes, Joe Hardy, Nick Herbert and Pedro Netto
Suggested Key: C
BPM: 150 (6/8)

Verse 1
    F
Flood us with Your presence
        Am   G
You're the God of majesty
    F
Fill the room with heaven
   Am   G
It's the air we long to breathe

Chorus
F
Spirit of the living God
Am
Fall on us
C
Fall on us
F
Spirit of the living God
Am   G
Fall on us we pray

Verse 2
Come and let it happen
Everything we long to see
Miracles and wonders
Every broken heart redeemed

Instrumental
F   Am   G

Bridge
F
Would you show us Your face
                   Am
As we sing, as we pray
      G
Fall on us again

Damares Gomes, Joe Hardy, Nick Herbert and Pedro Netto
© 2022 Capitol CMG Genesis/Safe And Sound Music (Admin. by Capitol CMG Publishing) ; Wings Music Group (Admin. by Sentric Music)

CCLI #: 7205327

Further resources for this song are available at
ccli.com/songbook

SongSelect is an indispensable resource.

- Lindsay Barr, Orchardhill Parish Church, Scotland.

SHEET MUSIC & LYRICS MADE EASY

SongSelect is your simple, single source of worship lyrics, chords, and sheet music. Transposable, customisable, and seamlessly accessible in your favourite presentation, planning, and worship software and apps.

SongSelect® by CCLI

Part of the CCLI family
Connected solutions for your worship

Sign up to SAVE 25% at ccli.com/family

CCLI Christian Copyright Licensing International. Registered in England & Wales: 2580472
Unit 16-17, Pacific House, 1 Easter Island Place, Eastbourne BN23 6FA, UK.

GOD OF THE AGES

9

Samuel Nwachukwu, Manor Collective, Sarah Bird, Elle Limebear
Suggested Key: C
BPM: 73 (4/4)

Verse 1
```
F                             C
Standing on the shoulders of my father's father's fathers
F                  C            G4
Living in the blessing of their prayers
F                     C
Kneeling down in reverence, in beautiful surrender
F           C         G4
Offering a sacrifice of praise
```

Chorus
```
        F               Gsus  G4
God of the ages, You never change
         Am7            G/B
Through generations You stay the same
```

Verse 2
Walking in the rhythm of the servant hearted mothers
Hours of devotion unto You
Raising up an army, a family of believers
Teaching them the way and the truth

Chorus 2
```
F                       Gsus  G4
God of the ages, You never change
         Am7            G/B
Through generations You stay the same
         Dm7         C/E
So I will bow down, so I will pray
              F2                G4
That our children's children, they'll do the same
```

Bridge
```
  (G#)   Am       F
I'll say  thank you Jesus
         C   G4
Every   day
```

Chorus 2 (Alt Chords)
```
           Dm7         C/E
God of the ages, You never change
         F2                G4
Through generations You stay the same
         Dm7         C/E
So I will bow down, so I will pray
              F2                G4
That our children's children, they'll do the same
```

Bridge (Alt Chords)
```
         Am7       Dm7
I'll say  thank you Jesus
    C/G  G4
Every   day
```

Verse 3
Resting in the promise of
Your goodness and your mercy
And Your faithfulness until the very end

Samuel Nwachukwu, Manor Collective, Sarah Bird, Elle Limebear
© Be Essential Songs / Limebear Project (Admin. by Essential Music Publishing LLC).
Remaining portion is unaffiliated.

CCLI #: 7208359

Further resources for
this song are available at
ccli.com/songbook

10 GOODNESS OF GOD

Ed Cash, Ben Fielding, Jason Ingram, Jenn Johnson, Brian Johnson
Suggested Key: A
BPM: 63 (4/4)

Verse 1
```
         A
I love you Lord
         D         A
Oh Your mercy never fails me
    E/G# F#m       D             A
All my   days, I've been held in Your hands
                  F#m    D
From the moment that I wake up,
            A  E/G#  F#m
Until I lay my head
       D      E       A
I will sing of the goodness of God
```

Chorus
```
D                        A
All my life You have been faithful
D                       A      E
All my life You have been so, so good
D                    A     E/G#  F#m
With every breath that I am able
       D      E       A
I will sing of the goodness of God
```

Verse 2
I love your voice
You have led me through the fire
In darkest night, you are close like no other
I've known you as a Father, I've known you as a friend
I have lived in the Goodness of God

Bridge
```
A/C#              D
  Your goodness is running after,
              E        A
It's running after me
A/C#              D              E        A
Your goodness is running after, it's running after me
              A              D
With my life laid down, I'm surrendered now,
              E       F#m
I give you everything
A/C#              D
  Your goodness is running after,
              E        A
It's running after me
```

Ed Cash, Ben Fielding, Jason Ingram, Jenn Johnson, Brian Johnson
© 2018 Capitol CMG Paragon (Admin. by Capitol CMG Publishing). Fellow Ships Music / So Essential Tunes (Admin. by Essential Music Publishing LLC). SHOUT! Music Publishing Australia (Admin. by SHOUT! Music Publishing UK). Bethel Music Publishing (Admin. by Song Solutions).

CCLI #: 7117726

Further resources for this song are available at
ccli.com/songbook

GRATITUDE

11

Benjamin Hastings, Brandon Lake and Dante Bowe
Suggested Key: G
BPM: 78 (6/8)

Verse 1
      G
All my words fall short
      Em
I've got nothing new
      D   C
How could I express all my gratitude

Verse 2
      G
I could sing these songs
      Em
As I often do
        D   C
But every song must end and You never do

Chorus
        G
So I throw up my hands and praise You
      D
again and again
                  C
'Cause all that I have is a hallelujah
Em   D
Hal-le-lujah
     G
And I know it's not much
                   D
But I've nothing else fit for a king
                  C
Except for a heart singing hallelujah
Em   D G
Hal-le-lu-jah

Verse 3
I've got one response
I've got just one move
With my arms stretched wide
I will worship You

Bridge
G
Come on my soul, Oh don't you get shy on me
G
Lift up your song,
G
'cause you've got a lion inside of those lungs
G
Get up and praise the Lord

G
Come on my soul, Oh don't you get shy on me
D
Lift up your song,
                             C
'cause you've got a lion inside of those lungs
                   G D
Get up and praise the Lord

G
Come on my soul, Oh don't you get shy on me
D
Lift up your song,
                             C
'cause you've got a lion inside of those lungs
                   Em D
Get up and praise the Lord

Benjamin Hastings, Brandon Lake and Dante Bowe
© 2019 SHOUT! Music Publishing Australia (Admin. by SHOUT! Music Publishing UK).
Bethel Music Publishing / Bethel Worship Publishing / Brandon Lake Music / Maverick City Publishing / Maverick City Publishing Worldwide (Admin. by Song Solutions).

CCLI #: 7158417

Further resources for this song are available at
ccli.com/songbook

12 GREATER THAN IT ALL (IT IS FINISHED)

Jake Isaac
Suggested Key: D
BPM: 70 (4/4)

Verse 1
```
              D    Dsus
I fix my eyes upon the cross
D                   Bm7
  Reaching out with all I've got
Bm7                A
  I'm letting go to start a - gain
G                      D
  I need Your love that's why I'm here
```

Verse 2
```
              D    Dsus
Waiting outside my life it calls
D                  Bm7
  So while I'm here I'll give my all
Bm7              A
  You are my peace within the storm
G                   D   Dsus D
  Here at the cross I find my home
```

Chorus
```
             G                       D   Dsus  D
You are greater, Jesus, You are greater than it all
             G                       Bm7
You are greater, Jesus, You are greater than it all
       A/C#
Than it all
              Em7
Grace and mercy found me
D/F#         G      A    Bm7
Oh, the blood of Jesus, is greater
              Em7
Grace and mercy found me
D/F#         G      A    D  Dsus D
Oh, the blood of Jesus, is greater
```

Verse 3
```
Lord, I believe You rose again
So I don't believe this is the end
You never fail, You have a plan
My life You hold within Your hands
```

Verse 4
```
So I'll walk by faith and not by sight
For You are my source, You are my light
In You I live, I will not die
You've stretched these wings, now I can fly
```

Bridge
```
             D
It is finished, it is finished
           Bm7                G
Jesus, You are greater than it all
                  D
Death couldn't hold You, You rose in power
           Bm7                G
Jesus, You are greater than it all
```

Jake Isaac
© 2014 Integrity Music (Admin. by Integrity Music Ltd)

CCLI #: 7030441

Further resources for this song are available at
ccli.com/songbook

HE'S ALIVE

Lou Fellingham, Nathan Fellingham and Emma Pears
Suggested Key: C
BPM: 97 (4/4)

Chorus
C   C/E Am
He's al-ive
            F   C
The Lord is risen
   G/B   Am Dm7
Oh Halle-lu-jah
              F/G G/C
My Saviour's risen
C   C/E Am
Now He reigns
      Fmaj7 C
In the heavens
   G/B   Am Dsus2/F#
Oh Halle-lu-jah
              F/G G/C
The Lord is risen

Verse 1
Am   Am/G   Dsus2/F#
   Remember when he told the disciples
        F   C   Bbmaj7 C#dmin
That he would be rising again?
   Dm9   C/E
Though crucified, Jesus now is alive
              Fmaj7   F/G Ab Bb
Don't seek the living among the dead

Verse 2
Lord over all, ascended in Glory
A brand new creation is here
Jesus is King, bring your worship to Him
Oh Father Your kingdom come on earth

Chorus 2
D/A   Gmaj9/B
He's al-ive
              Em7   Dmaj7
The Lord is risen
           Bm   Em7
Oh Halle-lu-jah
                    Bmaj7   Cmaj7
My Saviour's risen
D   D/F#   Bm
Now He reigns
        G   D
In the heavens
       A/C# Bm   Em9
Oh Halle-lu-jah
              G/A D
The Lord is risen

Bridge
D   C#m7   F#7
Hallelujah Christ is risen, There's an empty grave
Bm7   Am7   C/D
Hallelujah Christ is risen, My debt is paid
Gmaj9
Hallelujah Christ is risen
              Em9   G/A
All glory be to God, be to God

Chorus 2
E   E/D Amaj7/C#   A   E
He's al - ive,   The Lord is risen
   B/D# C#m F#m9   A/B E
Oh Halle - lu - jah,   My Saviour's ri-sen
E   E/G# F#sus2/A#   G#sus2/B# C#m
Now He   reigns   In the heav - ens
      Bm7   A F#m7   A/B D/E
Oh Halle-lu-jah   The Lord is ri sen
         C#m F#m11   A/B D/E
Oh Halle - lu - jah   The Lord is ri-sen
         C#m F#m7   A/B   E
Oh Halle - lu - jah   The Lord is ri-sen

Lou Fellingham, Nathan Fellingham and Emma Pears
© 2022 Freedom Sounds (Admin. By Song Solutions www.songsolutions.org)/
Remaining portion is unaffiliated.

CCLI #: 7194235

14 HOLY FOREVER

Brian Johnson, Chris Tomlin, Jason Ingram, Jenn Johnson, Phil Wickham
Suggested Key: A (G Capo 2)
BPM: 72 (4/4)

Verse 1
```
    G                  C                    G
A thousand generations falling down in worship
    Em           D (add4)   C2
To sing the song of ages to the Lamb
    G
And all who've gone before us,
C            G
and all who will believe
    Em          D(add4)     C2
Will sing the song of ages to the Lamb
```

Pre-Chorus
```
     C2          Em
Your Name is the highest,
    D(add4)
Your Name is the greatest
        Em              C2
Your Name stands above them all
    C2            Em
All thrones and dominions,
              D(add4)
all powers and positions
        Em                    Am7
Your Name stands above them all
```

Chorus 1
```
                   C2  Em D(add4)
And the angels cry:  ho - ly
                G/B  Em
All creation cries:  ho - ly
            Am7    D(add4)
You are lifted high, ho - ly
     G    Gsus. G
Holy forever
```

Verse 2
If you've been forgiven and if you've been redeemed
Sing the song forever to the Lamb
And if you walk in freedom, if you bear His Name
Sing the song forever to the Lamb
Sing the song forever and Amen

Chorus 2
With all the angels cry holy
All creation cries holy
You are lifted high, holy
Holy forever

Hear Your people sing holy
And to the King of kings, holy
And You will always be holy
Holy forever

Bridge
Your Name is the highest,
Your Name is the greatest
Your Name stands above them all
Above all thrones and dominions,
and all powers and positions
Your Name stands above them all

Outro
```
                      Am7    D(add4)
You will always be   ho - ly
         G    Gsus   G
Holy forever
```

Brian Johnson, Chris Tomlin, Jason Ingram, Jenn Johnson, Phil Wickham
© Phil Wickham Music / Simply Global Songs (Admin. by Small Stone Media BV, Holland (Admin. in the UK/Eire by Song Solutions www.songsolutions.org)). Capitol CMG Paragon / S. D. G. Publishing (Admin. by Capitol CMG Publishing). Be Essential Songs / My Magnolia Music (Admin. by Essential Music Publishing LLC). Bethel Music Publishing / Brian and Jenn Publishing (Admin. by Song Solutions).

CCLI #: 7201044

Further resources for this song are available at ccli.com/songbook

HONESTY

15

Benjamin Hastings, Elle Limebear and Jeff Pardo
Suggested Key: F
BPM: 66 (4/4)

Verse 1
Bbmaj7   Dm
You know where I've been
      C6   Bbmaj7
'cause You were there as well
              Dm   C6   Bbmaj7
You know who I'll be,   before I get there
Bbmaj7   Dm
You know what's hidden
      C6   Bmaj7
The shame behind the veil
              Dm
You know the real me
            C6   Bmaj7
When I don't know myself

Chorus
Bbmaj7
I've tried, I've tried,
     Dm   C
To be the way the world would want me
Bbmaj7
It's time, it's time,
       Dm   C
To believe the words You wrote about me
Gm   Bbmaj7   F   C
I won't live my life for appearance sake or masquerade
        Bbmaj7
You've made me to be me
    Dm   C6   Bmaj7 Dm C6
So I'll live honestly

Verse 2
I know You're making me new day after day
Heavenly Father your truth will set me free
I know there's power in every word you say
So fear will not hold me and guilt is not my name

Bridge
Bbmaj7
I'll bring my heart into the open
F/A   C
Give You my secrets, You already know them
Bbmaj7   F/A   C
You love me regardless, You love me as I am
Bbmaj7
I'll give my life, won't let it be stolen
F/A   C
Bring You my worship leave no words spoken
Bbmaj7
I love You, I love You, I love you
              F/A C
With all that I am

Outro
Bbmaj7
You made me to be me
Dm   C
So I'll live honestly
Bbmaj7   Dm   C Bbmaj7
If You want honesty, I'll live honestly

Benjamin Hastings, Elle Limebear and Jeff Pardo
© 2020 Da Bears Da Bears Da Bears Music /Meaux Jeaux Music (Admin by Capitol CMG Publishing;Be Essential Songs/Limebear Project (admin by Essential Music Publishing); SHOUT! Music Publishing Australia (Admin by SHOUT! Music Publishing UK)

CCLI #: 7147747

Further resources for this song are available at
ccli.com/songbook

16 HYMN OF THE SAVIOUR

Alanna Glover and Philip Percival
Suggested Key: C
BPM: 120 (3/4)

Verse 1
```
        Am      F        C          G
From the chaos of darkness, your word shaped the earth
        Am     F      C
In your image a people made
        Am      F       C       G
But we traded perfection, the truth for a lie
        Am      F       C
And your glory was veiled in shame
        F     C       G         Am
But a promise made, a blessing you gave,
        F    C     G
To a people of your name
        F        C       Em    Am
For this broken world, a Saviour foretold
        F      G    F     Am    C
To bear all our grief and pain
```

Verse 2
When the heavenly saviour descended his throne
All my sin on his shoulders laid
And to win our redemption, he suffered and died
For the sake of my guilt and shame
Oh the price he paid in taking my place
So that death was overcome
When the King of love burst forth from the grave
Proclaiming the victr'y won

Verse 3
At the end of the ages, the world passed away
I will gaze on my saviour's face
When my heart is perfected and free from my sin
I will rest in your glorious grace
For the song we raise, the works of our hands
Are in service of the King
When a thousand tongues cry, 'Glory to God'
Forever his praise we'll sing

Alanna Glover and Philip Percival
©2019 Percival, Philip (Admin. by Philip Gordon Percival). Glover, Alanna.

CCLI #: 7134330

Further resources for this song are available at ccli.com/songbook

SPRING HARVEST 2024

Skegness 1–5 April
Minehead 8–12 April

UP AND ALIVE

LIVING THE LIFE WE ARE MADE FOR

Scan Me

Booking launches 14 June 2023

17 I SPEAK JESUS

Abby Benton, Carlene Prince, Dustin Smith, Jesse Reeves, Kristen Dutton, Raina Pratt
Suggested Key: E
BPM: 74 (4/4)

Verse 1
E   Esus   E
I just want to speak the Name of Jesus
C#m7
Over ev'ry heart and ev'ry mind
       A2
'Cause I know there is peace within Your presence
            E
I speak Jesus

Verse 2
I just want to speak the Name of Jesus
'Til ev'ry dark addiction starts to break
Declaring there is hope and there is freedom
I speak Jesus

Chorus
             B   E/G#   A
Your Name is power, Your name is healing
              Esus E
Your Name is life
             B   E/G#   A
Break every stronghold, shine through the shadows
          E
Burn like a fire

Verse 3
I just want to speak the Name of Jesus
Over fear and all anxiety
To every soul held captive by depression
I speak Jesus

Bridge
              E
Shout Jesus from the mountains
 Esus   E
Jesus in the streets
C#m7
Jesus in the darkness over ev'ry enemy
A
Jesus for my family
                          E
I speak the Holy Name Jesus

Abby Benton, Carlene Prince, Dustin Smith, Jesse Reeves, Kristen Dutton, Raina Pratt
© 2019 Here Be Lions Publishing / Integrity's Praise! Music (Admin. by Integrity Music Ltd). BEC Worship (Admin. by Song Solutions). Raina Pratt publishing designee / Worship Coalition Songs / WriterWrong Music (Admin. by Song Solutions www.songsolutions.org).

CCLI #: 7136201

Further resources for this song are available at
ccli.com/songbook

JUSTICE

Luke Finch and Ali McFarlane
Suggested Key: B (G capo 4)
BPM: 79 (4/4)

Chorus
```
    D          G/B
You rule, You reign
    C2                      G
Let justice like a river roll again
    D          G/B
You rule, You reign
    C2                      G
Let justice like a river roll again
```

Verse 1
```
            C2                      G/B
You're the God who feeds five thousand hungry people
    C2                      G/B
Who stops the guilty stranger being stoned
            C2          D/F#    Em
You're the God who judges us as with fire
    C2          D/F#    G
The justice that you bring is merciful
```

Verse 2
You're the God who dethrones kings and exiles nations
Whose judgement is the path that leads us home
You're the God who speaks His word from the fire
The justice that you bring is powerful
The justice that you bring is powerful

Bridge
```
      D                Em7
The fire and the flood are reconciling us
      C2         G
To the God is sovereign
              D           Em7
The famine and the feast are returning you and me
      C2         G
To the God who is sovereign
```

Verse 3
You're the God who hears the song of the forgotten
Who liberates the captive and the slave
You're the God who walks with us in the fire
The justice that you bring is here today
The justice that you bring is here today

Tag
```
      G        Gsus4       G
Roll again, roll again, roll again
      G        Gsus4       G
Roll again, roll again, roll again
      Em7       D/F#       G
Roll again, roll again, roll again
      Em7       D/F#       G
Roll again, roll again, roll again
```

Luke Finch and Ali McFarlane
© 2022 Wings Music Group (Admin. by Sentric Music)

CCLI #: 7214805

Further resources for this song are available at
ccli.com/songbook

19 KINGDOM COME
(LIFT UP YOUR HEADS)

Rich Di Castiglione
Suggested Key: D
BPM: 73 (4/4)

Verse 1
D   D/F#   Bm
Earth is groaning and we are longing
                    G
for Your kingdom to come
D   D/F#   Bm   G
All creation and all of Heaven join their voices as one

Chorus
D   Dsus4
God let Your kingdom come
              D
May Your will be done
                Dsus4
God let Your kingdom come

Verse 2
Hope is stirring, joy arising as we look to the day
When all injustice will bow and every voice will cry out
Holy is Your name

Bridge
         D   Dsus4
Lift up your heads all the weak and the poor
             D   Dsus4
The Lord is at hand and His Kingdom is yours
             D   Dsus4
Lift up your hearts all who suffer and mourn
             D   Dsus4
The Lord is at hand and His Kingdom is yours
             D   Dsus4
Lift up your eyes all who hunger for more
             D   Dsus4
The Lord is at hand and His Kingdom is Yours
         Bm   G
Lift up a shout let the Earth hear your voice
             D/F#   A
The Lord is at hand and His Kingdom is yours

Rich Di Castiglione
© 2016 KXC Publishing (Admin. by Capitol CMG Publishing)

CCLI #: 7055441

LEAN IN

◆ 20

Lou Fellingham and Nathan Fellingham
Suggested Key: C
BPM: 76 (6/8)

Verse 1
```
C                    Dm              C
God of faithfulness, through the ages,
Am                      F
Grace and love filling history's pages
C             Dm
Breathing life into your creation,
C     Am                       F
Proving steadfast through generations
G    Am  C/E   F
Father, Spi – rit, Son
```

Chorus
```
         G  Am    F          C
So I'll lean in,  into your sovereignty,
  G   Am     F          C
Lean in and trust you again
      G    Am      F           C
All of my plans, I place in your hands
   Dm  Am      F               C
As I lean in and trust you, trust you again
```

Verse 2
Through uncertainty You are certain,
You're the rock where I lay my burden
You've been with me in joy and sorrow,
You will guide me through my tomorrow
Working for my good

Bridge
```
C
You will always provide,
        G/C           Dm
You continue to be my supply Lord
C
In your love I'll remain
      G/C                Dm
As I trust you again in your time Lord

        C
Father Your kingdom come
                G              Dm
And let Your will be done in my life Lord
        C
By your grace I will say,
                  G              Dm
"Surely Yours is the way I will follow!"
```

Lou Fellingham and Nathan Fellingham
© 2022 Freedom Sounds (Admin. by Song Solutions www.songsolutions.org)

CCLI #: 7206866

Further resources for this song are available at
ccli.com/songbook

21 LET EVERYTHING THAT HAS BREATH PRAISE

Hudson Virgo, Josh Tibbert, Neal Glanville, Sarah Teibo, Tom Endersby
Suggested Key: E
BPM: 115 (4/4)

Verse 1
A   C#m B
    Lord we gather   here in Your presence
A   C#m B
    As we come, we offer up our praises
A   C#m B
    For all You have done and all You will do
   C#m   B   Dmaj7
We lift our praise to You

Verse 2
Every tribe and generation
Raise your voice and come in celebration
At His throne we join with all creation
We lift our praise to You

Chorus 1
E
Let everything that has breath praise
B
Let everything that has breath praise the Lord
A
Let everything that has breath praise
    E/G#
We pour out our praise
     B
Jesus you are worth it all

Chorus 2
E
Let everything that has breath praise
D
Let everything that has breath praise the Lord
A
Let everything that has breath praise
    E/G#
We pour out our praise
     B
Jesus you are worth it all

Chorus 3
Hallelujah God be praised
Hallelujah God be praised
Hallelujah God be praised
We pour out our praise
Jesus you are worth it all

Chorus 4
As we worship fill this place
As we worship fill this place
As we worship fill this place
We pour out our praise
Jesus you are worth it all

Hudson Virgo, Josh Tibbert, Neal Glanville, Sarah Teibo, Tom Endersby
© 2022 Glanville, Neal / Teibo, Sarah (Admin. by Sentric Music).
Remaining portion is unaffiliated.

CCLI #: 7204108

Further resources for this song are available at
ccli.com/songbook

LORD WE PRAY FOR PEACE

Ben Slee, Sam Brewster, Thomas Brewster
Suggested Key: C
BPM: 70 (4/4)

Verse 1
```
C       F/C     Gsus4 G    F/A     G/B    C
Lord we pray for peace    to heal our fractured world
C          Dm7    G  Am       F      G   C
Send Your love to conquer where darkness overwhelms
G    Am   F  C/E  G     Am7       F
Jesus full of mercy, Hear our anguished plea
C        Dm7      G       Am
Prince of Peace and Lord of Love
     F      G     C
We pray to You for peace
```

Chorus
```
        Am         F
Have mercy, Lord Jesus
     C    Csus4  Gsus4    G
We cry to You    today
      C/E        F
Have mercy Lord Jesus
         Am  Dm7   Gsus4. G    C
Have mercy on us Lord,    we pray
```

Verse 2
Lord we pray for peace where lives are torn apart
Hope of every nation, restore each broken heart
Jesus Rock and Refuge, comfort those who flee
Master of the raging storm
We pray to You for peace

Verse 3
Lord we pray for peace where fear is all around
May Your love enfold us, may faith and hope abound
Jesus Lord and Victor, come and set us free
Saviour who has crushed the grave
We pray to You for peace

Ben Slee, Sam Brewster, Thomas Brewster
© 2022 Joyful Noise Music (Admin. by Sam Brewster). Joyful Noise Music (Admin. by Thomas Brewster). Slee, Ben.

CCLI #: 7193424

Further resources for this song are available at
ccli.com/songbook

23 LOVE AROUND

Samuel Nwachukwu
Suggested Key: A
BPM: 102 (4/4)

Intro
D2   F#m7   Esus   D2/B
D2   F#m7   Esus

Verse 1
A   A2/F#   Esus   D2
I've been searching, searching far and wide
A   A2/F#   Esus   D2
For love that could only be found in You
A   A2/F#   E   D2
Perfect always,   is Your unfailing love
A   A2/F#   E F#m   D2   Bm7
It's all in   You,   my Jesus, oh
A2/F#   Esus   D2   E   A/E   Esus
Never changing, never failing, oh

Chorus
          D   F#m7
Your Love is all around,
E   Bm7   D   F#m7
Around, around,   around, around
           E
You never let me go
           D   F#m7
You've turned my life around
E   Bm7   D   F#m7
Around, around,   around, around
           E
You never let me go

Bridge
          D2   E
All of my scars, all of my pain
          A2/F#   E/G#
All my mistakes, You've washed away
A   Bm7
Got me singing like oh
A/C#   D2   D2/E
Never changing, never failing

Chorus 2
          Eb   Gm7
Your Love is all around,
F   Cm7   Eb   Gm7
Around, around,   around, around
           F
You never let me go
           Eb   Gm7
You've turned my life around
F   Cm7   Eb   Gm7
Around, around,   around, around
           F
You never let me go

Outro
Eb   Gm7   F(4)   Eb2/C
Eb   Gm7   F(4)

Samuel Nwachukwu
© 2018 HFP Music (Admin. by HFP Music Limited).

CCLI #: 7174694

LOVE WON'T STOP

Brenton Brown, Nick Herbert, Tim Hughes, Jimmy James
Suggested Key: G
BPM: 115 (4/4)

Verse 1
G/B   C   D   Em
Everlasting ever strong
   G/B   C   D   Em
God Your love goes on and on
G/B   C
Time and again
    D   Em   G/B C D Em
We've known Your kindness

Verse 2
G/B   C   D   Em
Peace that lasts beyond the night
   G/B   C   D   Em
Hope that never leaves a fight
G/B   C
Always the same
    D   Em   G/B C D Em
Your love surrounds us

Chorus
C
Faithful in the fire
G
Faithful in the flood
         Em
Your love keeps coming
      D
It won't give up
C
Faithful in the battle
          Em
You are strong enough
     G/B   C
Your love won't stop

Verse 2
G
God Your goodness never sleeps
There's no promise You won't keep
Time and again You stand beside us

Bridge
G
Thank You for the heavens that are open wide
G
Thank You for the river that will not run dry
Cmaj7
Thank You for the blessing that is over my life
Cmaj7
Over my life over my life
Em
Thank You that You're faithful in the mystery
G
Thank You that You're working when I cannot see
Cmaj7
Thank You that Your love has got a hold on me
C   Am7
Hold on me hold on me

Brenton Brown, Nick Herbert, Tim Hughes, Jimmy James
© Capitol CMG Genesis / Generous Giver Music / Safe and Sound Music (Admin. by Capitol CMG Publishing). Integrity Music / Thankyou Music / Tim Hughes Designee (Admin. by Integrity Music Ltd).

CCLI #: 7143862

Further resources for this song are available at ccli.com/songbook

We have no musicians. The Prime App has made all the difference!

- Norma Mireless-Smith, USA.

TRACKS FOR WORSHIP MADE EASY

Short of musicians? Want a fuller sound? Loop Community provides customisable backing tracks, known as multitracks, and the free Prime multitracks app to play them, plus the support you need to get started.

Loop | **Part of the CCLI family**
Connected solutions for your worship

Sign up to SAVE 25% at ccli.com/family

CCLI Christian Copyright Licensing International. Registered in England & Wales: 2580472
Unit 16-17, Pacific House, 1 Easter Island Place, Eastbourne BN23 6FA, UK.

MAKE ROOM

Evelyn Heideriqui, Josh Farro, Lucas Cortazio, Rebekah White
Suggested Key: G
BPM: 63 (4/4)

Verse 1
G   D4
Here is where I lay it down,
              Am7
Every burden, every crown
              Cmaj7
This is my surrender,   this is my surrender
G   D4
Here is where I lay it down
              Am7
Every lie and every doubt
              C2
This is my surrender

Chorus
              G   D
And I will make room for You
              Am7
To do whatever you want to
         C2
To do whatever you want to
              G   D
And I will make room for you
              Am7
To do whatever you want to,
         C2
To do whatever you want to

Bridge
G
Shake up the ground of all my tradition
D
Break down the walls of all my religion
Am7
Your way is better,
C2
Your way is better

Ending
Here is where I lay it down
You are all I'm chasing now
This is my surrender, this is my surrender

2018 Evelyn Heideriqui, Josh Farro, Lucas Cortazio, Rebekah White
© 2018 A New Song For A New Day Music / Community Music Songs / Curb Congregation Songs / Curb Songs / Father of Lights Publishing (Admin. by Curb Music Publishing).

CCLI #: 7122057

26. MAKER OF THE MOON

John Mongan, Jonny Bird, Sarah Bird, Lydia McAllister, Elle-Anna Smith,
Josh Gale, Holly Roe, Jack Stimson, Martin Smith, Myles Dhillon
Suggested Key: A
BPM: 65 (4/4)

Verse 1
    F#m E   A
Hello maker of the moon
    Bm   A   E
Your creation has inspired my every move
    F#m E   A
You're the science in the stars
      Bm   A   E
There is beauty, there is fire in Your eyes

Chorus
      D   F#m
Here we are, face to face
  A   E
Lost in wonder at the God of time and space
  D   F#m
The universe declares your praise
  A   E
Singing holy, holy is your name

Verse 2
Hello tamer of the tides
Every day You're moving deeper in my life
You're the wildness in the wind
And I feel You so much closer than my skin

Bridge
                    D
I can feel Your heartbeat beating
                A/C#
I can hear my God is speaking
          E   F#m
King of creation, breathe upon me
                  D
You can hear my heartbeat beating
             A/C#
You can hear my spirit screaming
      E   F#m
King of creation, You amaze me

Verse 3
Hello maker of the moon
You were there when I was in my mother's womb

John Mongan, Jonny Bird, Sarah Bird, Lydia McAllister, Elle-Anna Smith,
Josh Gale, Holly Roe, Jack Stimson, Martin Smith, Myles Dhillon
© 2017 Be Essential Songs / Limebear Project (Admin. by Essential Music Publishing LLC).
Bright City Collective Ltd (Admin. by Integrity Music Ltd). Bespoke Records. Gloworks
Publishing Limited.

CCLI #: 7087139

Further resources for this song are available at
ccli.com/songbook

MORE THAN ENOUGH

April Ballard, Mat Miles and Robin Mitchell
Suggested Key: E
BPM: 75 (4/4)

Verse 1
C#m   G#m   A
I am in Your hands and I belong to You
                           B   C#m
You called me back when I was far from You
                    G#m
You drove away the darkness
                        A
Clothed me with your light, called me Your child

Chorus
              A   E   B
God You are good and Your mercy is forever
          G#m   C#m
I'm overwhelmed by the weight of Your love
            F#m   B
Your glory goes far beyond all my horizons
            G#m   C#m   B
You are all I need You are more than enough

Verse 2
Now I stand before You righteous and renewed
You gave Your life to bring me back to You
The path I used to follow is no longer my own
You lead me home

Bridge
C#m
Guilt you're not my partner
A
Shame you're not my friend
E
Death you're not my sentence
B
I don't stand condemned
C#m
Peace you are my promise
A
Truth you've set me free
E   B
Life in all its fullness is waiting for me

April Ballard, Mat Miles and Robin Mitchell
© 2023 Elevation (Admin. by Elevation www.songsolutions.org)

CCLI #: 7214797

28 ONE PEOPLE

Philippa Hanna, Isak Peterson, Nate Gardner
Suggested Key: C
BPM: 75 (4/4)

Verse 1
  C5   G5
One Church, one heart, one truth, one bride
 Am   F5
One body, that's who we are
C/E   C5/F   Gsus4 G C
 We stand together as one people under God
  C   Gadd4
The Father, the Son, the Spirit, three-in-one
      Am   F
Our firm foundation, the Cornerstone
C/E   G   Gsus4 G C
 We stand together as one people under God

Chorus 1
C   F C/E G
 Bring us closer to Your heart
        F C/E G
 Bring us back to where we started
       F   C/E   Gadd4
 As we gather at the cross, remind us who we are
     C5
One people under God

Verse 2
As we stand in one accord
All will confess that You are Lord
Our precious Saviour, You paid it all
We give You glory as one people under God

Bridge
Am   F
 Where there's unity, there is blessing
C/E   Gadd4
 Bring revival, bring revival
Am   F
 And You will find a bride, ready for a King
C/E   Gadd4
 Let Your Church arise [Repeat]
      C/E   F   G Am
(second chorus) Let Your Church arise, Jesus
C/E   F   Gsus4
 Let Your Church arise

Bridge 2
     Gm7/D C/E   G
And we'll see Your kingdom come
           F C/E G
As we praise Your name forever
           F
Til the day that You return,
    C/E   Gadd4
Lord, let Your will be done
         C5 Csus4 C
One people under God

Tag
 Csus4 C Csus4 C
We'll see Your kingdom come
      Gsus4 G
Lord, let Your will be done
      G   F
Til the day that You return,
   C/E   G
Lord, let Your will be done
         C
One people under God

© Philippa Hanna, Isak Peterson, Nate Gardner
2022 Integrity Music (Admin. by Integrity Music Ltd). Remaining portion is unaffiliated.

CCLI #: 7206977

Further resources for this song are available at
ccli.com/songbook

PRAYER OF CONSECRATION

29

Jonny Riggs, Rich di Castiglione
Suggested Key: E
BPM: 75 (4/4)

Verse 1
Amaj7   C#m7   B
Hear my pray'r of consecration, have my heart again
Amaj7   C#m7   B
All of me upon the altar: mind and soul and strength

Verse 2
Light the fire that I remember burned within my soul
Rekindle these fading embers, holy flame of love

Chorus
A   B   C#m   B/D#
Spirit, breathe upon this altar
E   B
Father, have my undivided heart
A   B   C#m   B/D#
Jesus, I surrender
E   B
All I want is to be set apart for You

Verse 3
In the shelter of Your mercy, I lay down my life
Ev'ry breath to offer up, a living sacrifice

Bridge
   A   G#m
My life to lift You high, my heart to bring You joy
    F#m   E
My hands to serve the ones You love, to comfort and restore
         A   G#m
You're worthy of my praise, You're worthy of my song
       F#m   E
You're worthy of my ev'rything, Jesus, have it all

Jonny Riggs, Rich di Castiglione
© 2021 Integrity Worship Music / Vineyard Songs (UK/Eire)
(Admin. by Integrity Music Ltd).

CCLI #: 7185118

Further resources for
this song are available at
ccli.com/songbook

30 PULL ME THROUGH

Damilola Makinde, Malcolm McCarthy, Rich di Castiglione
Suggested Key: F# (D Capo 4)
BPM: 74 (4/4)

Verse 1
```
      D                  Em        G
When I can't see what's in front of me
      Bm            A          G
You hold my hand and guide my feet
       D              Em          G
Your word is a lamp that lights my way
             Bm             A          G
You're the fire by night and the cloud by day
```

Chorus
```
                    G         D/F#
I've never known another like You
               Em              D/F#
No other God can do the things You do
                       G              D/F#
Through every single valley, mountain
                       Em         D
Drought or fountain, You pull me through
```

Verse 2
You sit me down and wash my feet
You're the God who loves to comfort me
The hands that hold the stars in place
Pull me into a warm embrace

Bridge
```
D
When I'm walking through the darkest valley
You pull me through
D
When I'm stranded by the lonely wayside
You pull me through
D
When my hope is faint and my heart's in pain
You pull me through
D
Whatever state that I am in, You pull me through

D
If you're walking through the darkest valley
He'll pull you through
D
If you're stranded by the lonely wayside
He'll pull you through
          Bm                G
If your hope is faint and your heart's in pain
D/F#         A
He'll pull you through
     Bm     A     G         D
Our God is able, He'll pull you through
```

Damilola Makinde, Malcolm McCarthy, Rich di Castiglione
© 2022 KXC Publishing (Admin. by Capitol CMG Publishing).

CCLI #: 7198484

Further resources for this song are available at ccli.com/songbook

RAISED WITH CHRIST

31

Joy Bishop, Tom Read and Jamie Thomson
Suggested Key: G
BPM: 80 (4/4)

Verse
```
G              Gsus4 G
The firstborn of all creation
Em7                  C
The world was made for Your delight
G               Gsus4 G
Taking on our human nature,
Em7             C   G/B
Becoming sin to give us life
```

Pre Chorus
```
C                 G
You hold everything together
Em7             D  G/B
From beginning to the end
C                   G
With a love no one can measure
Em7                D
Stronger than the grip of death
```

Chorus
```
         G
I've been raised with Christ
         D           Em7
The old has gone the new has come to life
    G/B         C  Em7 D
I will lift my voice and sing Your praise
   G/B       C  Em7 D
Forever I will sing Your praise
```

Verse 2
I fix my eyes upon the heavens
I set my mind on things above
You are the prize, You are my treasure
How sweet the name that rescues us

Bridge
(Pedal G first time through)
```
                              G
We have found our freedom, we are free indeed,
                       G
The empty grave is our victory
                       G
Our sin is cancelled, He has nailed it to the cross,
                    G
The King of heaven is alive in us
```

Bridge (repeat)
```
         Em           D/F#    G
We have found our freedom, we are free indeed,
       C               G
the empty grave is our victory
         Em           D/F#    G
Our sin is cancelled, He has nailed it to the cross,
                    C          D    G
the King of heaven is alive in us
```

Joy Bishop, Tom Read and Jamie Thomson
© 2019 Bespoke Records

CCLI #: 7118133

Further resources for this song are available at
ccli.com/songbook

32 SAME GOD

Brandon Lake, Chris Brown, Pat Barrett, Steven Furtick
Suggested Key: D
BPM: 73 (4/4)

Verse 1
D   G/D   D
 I'm calling on the God of Ja - cob
D   G/D   D
 Whose love endures through genera - tions
Bm   G
 I know that You will keep Your covenant
D   G/D   D
 I'm calling on the God of Mo - ses
D   G/D   D
 The one who opened up the o - cean
Bm   G   D
 I need You now to do the same thing for me

Chorus
D   A/C#
 O God, my God, I need You
Bm   A   G
 O God, my God, I need You now
         D/F#   G   A
 How I need You now
D   A/C#
 O Rock, O Rock of ages
Bm   A   G
 I'm standing on Your faithfulness
D/F   G   A
 On Your faithfulness

Verse 2
I'm calling on the God of Mary
Whose favour rests upon the lowly
I know with You all things are possible
I'm calling on the God of David
Who made a shepherd boy courageous
I may not face Goliath
But I've got my own giants

Bridge
D
 You heard Your children then
Bm
 You hear Your children now
G   D/F#   G   A
 You are the same God, You are the same God

You answered prayers back then
And You will answer now
You are the same God, You are the same God

You were providing then
You are providing now
You are the same God, You are the same God

You moved in power then
God move in power now
You are the same God, You are the same God

You were a healer then
You are a healer now
You are the same God, You are the same God

Bm
 You were a Savior then
D/A
 You are a Savior now
Gb   D/F#   G   Em
 You are the same God, You are the same God

Final Verse/Outro
D   G/D   D
 I'm calling on the Holy Spi - rit
D
 Almighty River come and
G/B   D/A G   D/F# D
 fill   me   a - gain

Brandon Lake, Chris Brown, Pat Barrett, Steven Furtick
© Capitol CMG Genesis / Housefires Sounds (Admin. by Capitol CMG Publishing). Music by Elevation Worship Publishing (Admin. by Essential Music Publishing LLC). Bethel Music Publishing / Brandon Lake Music / Maverick City Publishing Worldwide (Admin. by Song Solutions).

Further resources for this song are available at ccli.com/songbook

CCLI #: 7183537

LET'S MAKE WAVES TOGETHER

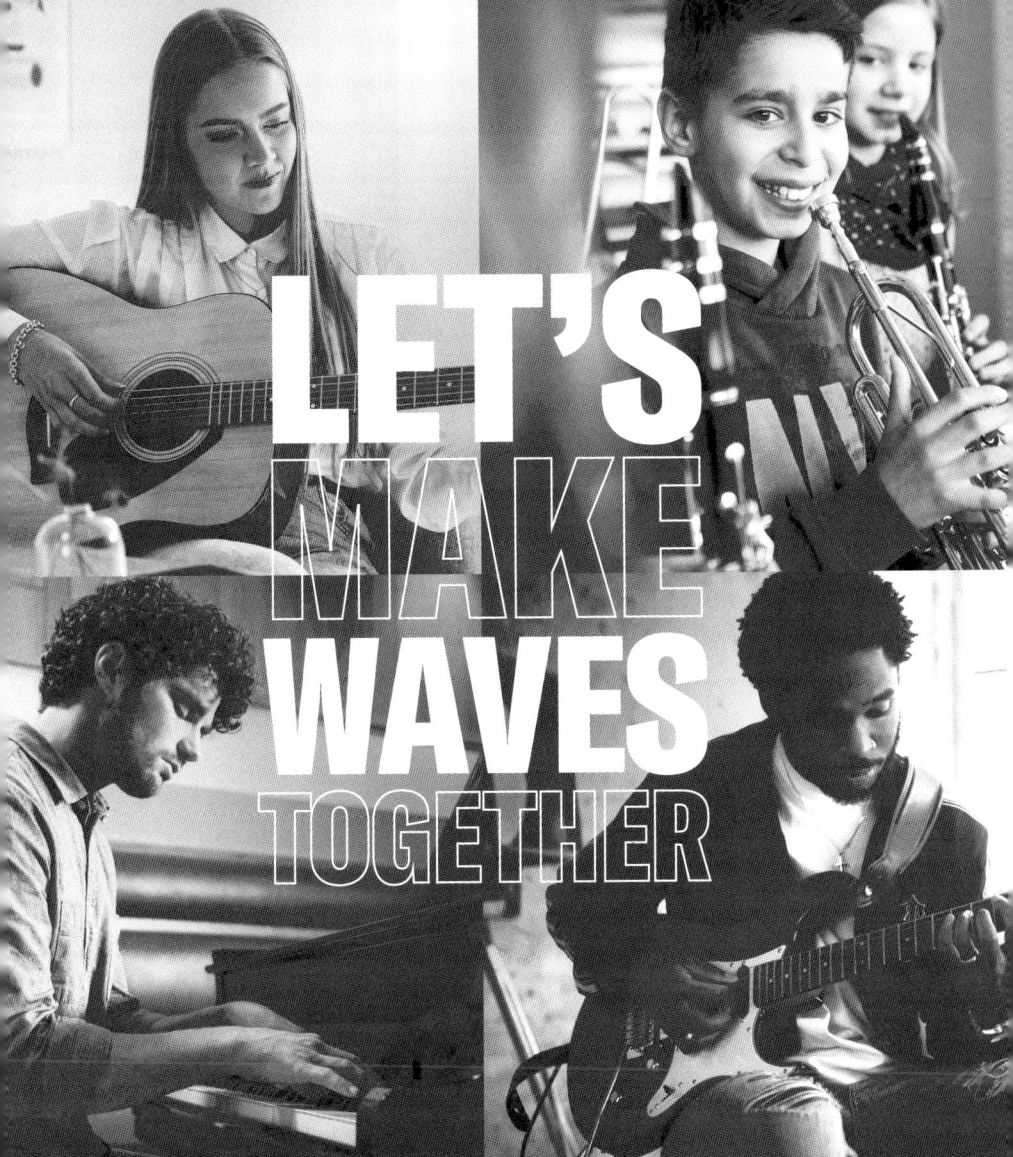

FIND OUT MORE AT YAMAHA MUSIC LONDON

worship@yamahamusiclondon.com

⚫ YAMAHA
Make Waves

33 SON OF SUFFERING

Aaron Moses, David Funk, Matt Redman, Nate Moore
Suggested Key: A
BPM: 71 (4/4)

Verse 1
  A
Oh, the perfect son of God
 Esus E
In all his innocence
  A/C#   D2 F#m7 E
Here walking in the dirt with you and me
  A
He knows what living is
   Esus   E
He's acquainted with our grief
 A/C#   D2 F#m7 E
A man of sorrows, son of suffering

Chorus
   Dmaj7
Blood and tears
   A
How can it be?
     E
There's a God who weeps
      F#m7
There's a God who bleeds
    Dmaj7
Oh, praise the one
    E F#m7
Who would reach for me
 E
Hallelujah
   D   A
To the son of suffering

Verse 2
Some imagine you
Are distant and removed
But you chased us down in merciful pursuit
To the sinner, you were grace
And the broken you embraced
And in the end, the proof is in your wounds
Oh, in the end, the proof is in your wounds

Bridge
A
Your cross, my freedom, Your stripes, my healing
A
All praise King Jesus, Glory to God in Heaven
A
Your blood, still speaking,
Your love, still reaching
        D
All praise King Jesus, Glory to God in Heaven

A   D/F#
Your cross, my freedom, Your stripes, my healing
A/C#   D
All praise King Jesus, Glory to God in Heaven
A
Your blood, still speaking,
D/F#
Your love, still reaching
A/C#   D
All praise King Jesus, Glory to God forever

Bridge 2
A   Bm
All praise King Jesus, All praise King Jesus
A/C#   D
All praise King Jesus, Glory to God in forever
A   Bm
All praise King Jesus, All praise King Jesus
F#m   D   A
All praise King Jesus, Glory to God forever

Aaron Moses, David Funk, Matt Redman & Nate Moore
© 2021 Maverick City Publishing / Mouth Of The River Music (Admin by Essential Music Publishing) Aaron Moses Chiriboga Music (Admin. by Essential Music Publishing LLC). Integrity Worship Music / Said And Done Music (Admin. by Integrity Music Ltd). Bethel Music Publishing / David Funk (Admin. by Song Solutions).

CCLI #: 7179241

Further resources for this song are available at ccli.com/songbook

THANK YOU

Josh Gauton and Tom Read
Suggested Key: A (G Capo 2)
BPM: 72 (4/4)

Verse 1

```
        G
When my words run out
       Em
Let my spirit sing
    C      Am
Thank You, thank you
   G
I cannot express
         Em
Just how much you mean to me
C      D     G
Thank you my Lord
```

Chorus 1

```
           C
For this world you made
       Em    D
With a single breath
            C    G    D
All your beauty woven through
                 C
For your love, so deep
        Em    D
Ever close to me
  C - D   G
I thank you
```

Chorus 2

For the debt you paid
On that borrowed cross
Where you died instead of me
For this life reborn
And the one to come
I thank you

Bridge

```
         C  G/B
Hallelu - jah
           D   Em
Hallelu - jah
               C       G/B
All my gratitude and praise
             D
Belongs to you
```

Josh Gauton and Tom Read
© 2019 Running Club Songs (Admin. by Integrity Music Ltd). Bespoke Records.

CCLI #: 7121015

Further resources for
this song are available at
ccli.com/songbook

35 WE SAY YES

Ian Yates, Sam Blake and Joel Pridmore
Suggested Key: G
BPM: 72 (4/4)

Verse 1
```
C          G       Em7 D  C       G        D
We choose to serve You,    to follow where you lead
C          G       Em7 D  C       G        D
To be Your witness,        to be Your hands and feet
```

Chorus 1
```
      C    G       Em7       D
We say Yes,    My soul says Yes
      C              G
Whatever You have for me
Em7          D
Whatever lies ahead
```

Tag
```
      C   G  Em7  D
We say Yes
```

Verse 2
In every season, we can trust in You
For You are with us, You are always good

Bridge
```
       C                D       Em7         G/B
We know that You are for us, not against us, not against us
       C                D       Em7         G/B
We know that You are for us, not against us, not against us
       C                D       Em7         G/B
We know that You are for us, not against us, not against us
       C                D       Em7   G/B
We know that You are for us, not against us
```

Chorus 2
```
C      G Em7  D
Hallelujah, hallelujah
C      G   Em7     D
Hallelujah, My soul says Yes
```

Ian Yates, Sam Blake and Joel Pridmore
© 2018 Elim Sound Publishing (Admin. by Song Solutions www.songsolutions.org).

CCLI #: 7106926

Further resources for this song are available at
ccli.com/songbook

WHAT A FRIEND WE HAVE IN JESUS

Joseph Scriven Medlicott, Pete James
Suggested Key: E (D Capo 2)
BPM: 90 (4/4)

Verse 1
```
D            A/C#    Bm7
What a friend we have in Jesus,
G          A        D
All our sins and griefs to bear!
         A    Bm    G       A    D
What a privilege to carry everything to God in pray'r!
D              A        Bm7
Oh, what peace we often forfeit,
G             A       D
Oh, what needless pain we bear,
         A   Bm7   G          A    D
All because we do not carry, everything to God in pray'r!
```

Chorus
```
         G              D
What a friend we have in Jesus,
         A            Bm7
What a friend we have in Him,
         G              D          Asus4  A
For he knows us and he holds us in his hands
         G              D
And his grace is never failing
         A            Bm7
and his love with out an end
         G              D
What a friend we have in Jesus
         A            D
What a friend we have in him
```

Verse 2
Blessed Saviour, you have promised,
You will all our burdens bear;
May we ever, Lord, be bringing,
all to you in earnest pray'r.
Soon in glory bright, unclouded,
there will be no need for pray'r —
Rapture, praise, and endless worship
will be our sweet portion there.

Verse 3
Have we trials and temptations?
Is there trouble anywhere?
We should never be discouraged,
Take it to the Lord in pray'r.
Can we find a friend so faithful
Who will all our sorrows share?
Jesus knows our every weakness;
Take it to the Lord in pray'r.

Joseph Scriven Medlicott, Pete James
© 2013 Elevation (Admin. by Elevation www.songsolutions.org)

CCLI #: 6542519

37 YOU ARE MY FATHER (CHILD OF GOD)

Ben Slee and Joe Smith
Suggested Key: G
BPM: 80 (6/8)

Verse 1

                  Bm
You called my name
  G   D   A
Before You formed the earth.
               Bm
You saw my frame,
G   D   A
 Knit me together with a word.
            G   D
You designed my heart to know You,
       A   Bm
Breathing life into my bones,
  G   D/F#   A
Forever You have loved me as Your own

Chorus

         G   D/F#
You are my Father, I am Your child.
         G   Bm   A
Loved and accepted, nothing could separate us now
         G   Bm D/F#
Adopted forever, purchased with blood.
     Gmaj7   A   D   G   D A
You are my Father and I am a child of God.

Verse 2

You know my need
before I ever call.
You guide my feet,
teach me to plant my steps in Yours.
And you comfort and protect me
with new mercies day by day.
You know my weakness, yet Your love remains.

Verse 3

And when I fall
and wander from Your ways
ashamed by it all,
fearing I've squandered all Your grace:
then I turn and see You running
with forgiveness in Your gaze
still I'm welcome in my Father's embrace!

Ben Slee and Joe Smith
© 2021 Slee, Ben. Remaining portion is unaffiliated.

CCLI #: 7199513

Further resources for
this song are available at
ccli.com/songbook

YOU ARE THE CHRIST

38

Olly Knight and Tom James
Suggested Key: G
BPM: 134

Verse 1
```
      G/B     C
Come and see the King,
         G      D
through the pages of his Word
         G/B        C
The God who walked on this earth,
         G      D
To serve and not be served
         G/B   Em
Crowds would gather to see,
     G/B          D
as the blind were given sight
         G/B         C
And hear the power of his voice
         G      D
As he raised the dead to life
```

Pre-Chorus
```
G/B  C         D      Em
We believe your Word is true
             C        Em       D
Your Spirit's opened our hearts to You
```

Chorus 1
```
           G
You're our Saviour, We'll forever sing your praise
Em
Jesus, name above all names
     C
Messiah, Son of God with power to save
Em              D
Lord we believe You are the Christ
```

Verse 2
```
Come and see the man,
who wore a crown of thorns
As He died on a cross
The weight of sin he bore
Now the author of life,
Is lifeless where he lays
But see the power of God
As He rises from the grave
```

Bridge
```
              C
We will tell of You
D        Em
All our hope in You
G/B   C                                   D
As we share your love speak through your Word
G/B    C     G/B  C
Spirit breathe anew
D        Em   D   Em
With our faith renewed
G/B         C              Em   D
May this nation turn to follow You
```

Olly Knight and Tom James
© 2018 Song Solutions Daybreak (Admin. by Song Solutions www.songsolutions.org)

Further resources for this song are available at
ccli.com/songbook

CCLI #: 7112230

39. YOU'RE STILL GOD

Jonny Bird, Matt Armstrong, Philippa Hanna, Tony Wood
Suggested Key: C
BPM: 78 (4/4)

Verse 1
                                    C
When all foundations have been shaken
                           Am
When I'm left standing in the dark
                         Gadd4
And all I feel is my heart breaking
                     F
You still reign and You're still God

Verse 2
                          C
And when it feels all hope has faded
                      Am
The heavy questions hit so hard
                         Gadd4
And though my soul may feel forsaken
                    C   Csus4
You still reign and You're still God

Chorus
C   F
  Though I can't see what's before me
                     Am
I know that I can trust Your heart
                       Gadd4
And this one truth will be my story
G7   C   Fsus2 C
  You still reign and You're still God

Verse 3
I will declare that You are with me
Though voices whisper that You're not
You'll never leave me nor forsake me
'cause You still reign and You're still God

Instrumental
Dm7 F Am G Dm7 F Am G

Verse 4
When my enemies surround me
I'll trust the victory of Your cross
And fix my eyes upon You, Jesus
For You are God and I am not

Chorus 2
C   F
You are good and You are faithful
                             Am
As You have been from the start
                               G
You work in all things for Your glory
G7   C   Fsus2 C
  You still reign and You're still God

Jonny Bird, Matt Armstrong, Philippa Hanna, Tony Wood
© 2020 Curb Wordspring Music / Eyes Up Songs (Admin. by Small Stone Media BV, Holland (Admin. in the UK/Eire by Song Solutions www.songsolutions.org)). Curb Congregation Songs / Tony Wood Songs (Admin. by Curb Music Publishing). Integrity Music (Admin. by Integrity Music Ltd). Remaining portion is unaffiliated.

CCLI #: 7147739

Further resources for this song are available at ccli.com/songbook

YOU RESTORE MY SOUL

40

Matt Fury, Lauren Harris and Tom Read
Suggested Key: G
BPM: 68 (4/4)

Verse 1
```
     G            C/G             G    C/G
The Lord is my shepherd,  He restores my soul
     G            C/G             G    C/G
He leads by still waters, He restores my soul
```

Pre-chorus
```
C          D         Em
Surely Your goodness and mercy
    G/B
Are chasing after me
 C                   D
All of the days of my life
```

Chorus
```
   C                       G
Even when I'm lost in the deepest valley
  D    Em
  I'll fear no evil
C                         G
  Even when the silence falls around me
D   Em          C
  I know you hear me
              G              D
Even when it feels like we're separated
         Em         C G  D
You're holding onto me
```

Verse 2
You lift my head, You wipe my tears,
You restore my soul
You draw me into Your embrace,
You restore my soul

Chorus 2
Even when I'm lost in the deepest valley
You're holding onto me
Even when the silence falls around me
You're holding onto me
Even when it feels like we're separated
You're holding onto me

Bridge
```
                       G   C/E
You restore my soul
                       G/D   C
You restore my soul
```

Matt Fury, Lauren Harris and Tom Read
© 2018 Bespoke Records and Integrity Music (Admin. by Integrity Music)

CCLI #: 7114848

Further resources for this song are available at
ccli.com/songbook

All-age Song Index

1	All Through History
2	Creator God
3	Giant Of Faith
4	God Is Good
5	God Suit On
6	I'm All In
7	King Of Me
8	Move
9	Oh What A Day
10	This Is The Kingdom

1 ALL THROUGH HISTORY

Becky Drake
Suggested Key: C
BPM: 126 (4/4)

Verse 1
```
C                            F  G
Noah built the most enormous boat
    C                        F  G
That kept the birds and animals afloat
   F        C       G/B      C
The Lord was good, the Lord was strong
    Am    F           |C  |F G| C  |F  G
And Noah lived his life for Him
```

Verse 2
Moses led his people through the sea
Taking them away from slavery
The Lord was good the Lord was strong
And Moses lived his life for Him

Chorus:
```
      F           C/E
Oh thank You, oh thank You
   Am              G
That all through history You were faithful
   F          C/E
Thank You, oh thank You
      Am              G              Dm       G
That You are just the same when it comes to me
                  C
When it comes to me
```

Verse 3
David fought Goliath and he won
A humble shepherd boy became a king
The Lord was good the Lord was strong
And David lived his life for Him

Verse 4
Daniel was inside a lion's den
But God brought him to safety once again
The Lord was good the Lord was strong
And Daniel lived his life for Him

Verse 5
Jesus died to take away our sin
So we could get to know our God again
The Lord is good the Lord is strong
And we will live our lives for Him

Becky Drake
© 2007 Song Solutions Daybreak (Admin. by Song Solutions www.songsolutions.org).

CCLI #: 5100206

Further resources for this song are available at
ccli.com/songbook

CREATOR GOD

◇ 2

Nick Drake and Becky Drake
Suggested Key: C
BPM: 112 (4/4)

Verse 1
```
              C         G/B
You put the stars in outer space
              Am        F
You put the freckles on my face
            F               C
And all the fish that swim and all the birds that fly
          G
Were made from Your incredible imagination
```

Chorus
```
C       G/B
Creator God, we're singing to the
   Am      F
Creator God of all the world
C       G/B           F
Creator God, we celebrate You
              C
We celebrate You
```

Verse 2
You spread the ripples through the sea
You painted stripes on every bee
And all the grass that grows and all the leaves that fall
Are part of Your amazing plans for this creation...

Verse 3:
You put the heat into the sun
You placed a heart in everyone
And all the music played and all the dancing done
Reminds us that we're made to be creative like...

Nick Drake and Becky Drake
© 2007 Song Solutions Daybreak (Admin. by Song Solutions www.songsolutions.org)

CCLI #: 5100172

Further resources for this song are available at
ccli.com/songbook

3. GIANT OF FAITH

Pete James
Suggested Key: G
BPM: 138 (4/4)

Verse 1
G   Em
We all come in different shapes and sizes
 Am   D
And life is full of many surprises
   G   Em
But one thing stays the same, Jesus is on my side
  Am   D
I don't need to be afraid, I don't need to run and hide

Pre-Chorus
   C G/B   Am   D
When I open my bible it's clear as can be
  G   D/F#   Em D
The God that I read about's with me
  Am   D
And I'm going to be a giant of faith

Chorus
    G
Like Moses (Moses)
And Joseph (Joseph)
       D/F#   Em
Daniel, Esther, Rahab and Ruth
  Em/D   C   D
No denying the truth, they're giants of faith
    G
Like David (David)
Elijah (Elijah)
      D/F#   Em
Noah and the rest of the team
Em/D C   D
I'm gonna be a giant of faith
   D
I'm gonna be a giant of faith

Verse 2
Everyday we always stick together
Hand in hand through every adventure
If I'm playing with my friends
Or when I go to sleep
I know You are always there
And angels are watching me

Verse 3
   Am   D
By faith I can do anything
   B/D#   Em
By faith I can do anything
   Am   D   F/G
By faith I can do anything through Christ

Pete James
© 2010 Elevation (Admin. by Elevation www.songsolutions.org)

CCLI #: 5120004

Further resources for this song are available at
ccli.com/songbook

GOD IS GOOD

◆ 4 ◆

Nick Drake and Becky Drake
Suggested Key: D
BPM: 112 (4/4)

Verse 1
```
G        D      Aadd4   Bm
  Here we are, people of faith
G            D       Bm        Aadd4
  Some with smiles, others with fears that they face
G         D      Aadd4  Bm          G  D  Aadd4
  Here we come, ready to bring who we are
```

Chorus
```
G      D   A  Bm   G     D      A
God is good,      God is good to us
G          D         A              Bm
All through time, every hour, every minute
           G    D    A
God is good,   God is good
```

Verse 2
Here we are, children of God
Family joining together as one
Here we come, ready to sing who You are

Bridge
```
         D
Oh, praise Him, for He is good
         D
Oh, praise Him, for He is good
     Bm  G              D   A
Oh, praise Him, for He is good
     Bm  G         Asus4  A
Oh, praise Him, for He is good
```

Tag
```
         D    G          D/F#   A
Oh, praise Him, for He is good
         Bm   G          D   A
Oh, praise Him, for He is good
         D    G          D/F#   A
Oh, praise Him, for He is good
         Bm   G          Asus4  A
Oh, praise Him, for He is good
         D
He is good
```

Nick Drake and Becky Drake
© 2022 Integrity Music Europe (Admin by Integrity Music ltd)

CCLI #: 7152585

Further resources for this song are available at
ccli.com/songbook

5 GOD SUIT ON

Pete James and Harvey Jessop
Suggested Key: G
BPM: 126 (4/4)

Verse 1
```
       C            G
Every morning when I wake
D        Em7
I get ready, I get ready
           C            G
Got my armour for the day (hey!)
D        Em7
I get ready, I get ready
```

Pre Chorus
```
C         D              Em7
This way, this way, I know you're with me
C       D     Em7
Every step I take, Whoaoaoh
C         D              Em7
This way, this way, I know you're with me
C     G     D
Every step I take
```

Chorus
```
        C              D      Em7
I got the sword of the Spirit, the shield of faith
         C      D         Em7
The belt of truth around my waist
            C         D      Em7
When I feel weak you make me strong
             C           D       Em7
Never back down, I got my God suit on
    Em7       D/F#      G
Your saving grace will guard my head
              C           D          Em7
Your righteousness like a bullet proof vest
              C        D      Em7
These good news shoes were made to run
             C           D       Em7
Never back down, I got my God suit on
             C           D       Em7
Never back down, I got my God suit on
```

Verse 2
```
Every battle that I face
I'll be ready, I'll be ready
When the arrows fly my way (hey!)
Hold me steady, hold me steady
```

Bridge
```
C    D   Em7
10, 9, 8, 7, 6
         C                    D          Em7
Got my hands in the air and your praise on my lip
C    D   Em7
5, 4, 3, 2, 1
                 C            D       Em7
Every battle I face my God has won
C    D   Em7
10, 9, 8, 7, 6
         C                    D          Em7
Got my hands in the air and your praise on my lip
C    D   Em7
5, 4, 3, 2, 1
             C           D       Em7
Never back down, I got my God suit on
```

Pete James and Harvey Jessop
© 2016 Song Solutions Daybreak / Swell Revolution
(Admin. by Song Solutions www.songsolutions.org). Jessop, Harvey

CCLI #: 7073873

Further resources for this song are available at
ccli.com/songbook

Easy to learn, 10/10.

- Charlie L, Tech Services, USA.

WORSHIP APPS MADE EASY

WorshipTools makes simple, feature-packed, and free software designed specifically to equip your worship team and enhance your worship services.

WorshipTools

Part of the CCLI family
Connected solutions for your worship

Find out more at ccli.com/family

CCLI Christian Copyright Licensing International. Registered in England & Wales: 2580472
Unit 16-17, Pacific House, 1 Easter Island Place, Eastbourne BN23 6FA, UK.

6 I'M ALL IN

Ian Yates, Sam Blake, Hilary Sanders and Sue Rinaldi
Suggested Key: A
BPM: 144 (Swung 8s)

Verse 1
```
        C5  A5         G5
There's a hope for the world
        D5              A5
When it feels like it's falling apart
                G5
There's a love that restores,
        D5              A5
Ev'ry city, ev'ry home, ev'ry heart
```

Pre-Chorus
```
A           G
Jesus is the One, mighty to save
        C           D
He's calling us to join his team today,
Won't you join in?
```

Chorus
```
A       G       D/F#  G     A
I'm all in, we're all in, we're all in this together
A       G       D/F#  G     A5
I'm all in, we're all in, we're all in this together
```

Verse 2
There's a call to join in
With my gifts I'm playing my part
There's a strength that's within
God's power inside of my heart

Bridge
```
C5      A           G
Team up! With the greatest hero
        F#m         G
Hands up! Who wants to help?
        A       G
Stand up! For the poor and hungry
C           D           A5
Come and be a part of God's action plan
        A       G
Team up! With the greatest hero
        F#m         G
Jump up! Who's ready to go?
        A       G
Speak up! For the lost and lonely
C           D           A5
Come and be a part of God's action plan
        C5      D       A5  D5  C5  A5  D5
To fix up this world with love
```

Tag
```
D5  C5     A5              D5   C5   A5
    Fix up!    This world with love
C5      A5              D5
Fix up!    This world with love
C5      A5      D5          Am   Asus4  A5
Fix up!    This world with love
```

Ian Yates, Sam Blake, Hilary Sanders and Sue Rinaldi
© 2022 Song Solutions Daybreak (Admin. by Song Solutions www.songsolutions.org)

CCLI #: 7192774

KING OF ME

⟨7⟩

Chris Llewellyn, Stephen Mitchell and Gareth Gilkeson
Suggested Key: G
BPM: 87 (4/4)

Chorus
G   C G
My God's the king of the giants
D   C G
My God's the king of the lions
Em7   C   G
My God's the king of the creatures of the deep
D   C G
My God's the King of me

Verse 1
           Em   C   G
Have you heard the story about my friend King Dave?
         Em   C   G
Wouldn't let the giant stand in his way
           G6   Am7   G/B
He said 'hand me my sling 'cause he's not that tall'
D   C   G
'My God is bigger and I'll watch him fall'

Verse 2
Have you heard the one about this guy called Dan?
Yes, he was a mighty holy praying man
They said 'throw him to the den of the scary beasts'
But God saved our hero from the lion's teeth

Bridge
D
This is more than history
Em   C
He will do the same for me
          D
Like Jonah and the whale at sea
          Em   C
When I'm lost and afraid all alone in the dark
         D   D
You're with me, oh, You're with me

Chris Llewellyn, Stephen Mitchell and Gareth Gilkeson
© 2019 Capitol CMG Paragon / Rend Family Music
(Admin. by Capitol CMG Publishing).

CCLI #: 7134317

Further resources for
this song are available at
ccli.com/songbook

8 MOVE

Nick Drake and Becky Drake
Suggested Key: E
BPM: 125 (4/4)

Verse 1
E   A/E   B/E   E A/E B/E
Open hands ask for You to come
E   A/E   B/E   E   A/E B/E
Open hearts wait for You to come

Pre-Chorus 1
  C#m   B/D#   E   A C#m B
My soul is longing for the Spirit of God to come
         C#m   B/D#   E   A E B/D
Yeah, we're all longing for the Spirit of God to come

Chorus
B   C#m
Move in my heart, move in my mind
A   E/G#   B
Pour Your love and power inside
B   C#m
Move in my day, move in my night
A   E/G#   B
You're the One I need in my life

Verse 2
When You come, I'll never be the same
In Your pow'r, I'm feeling brave again

Pre-Chorus 2
  C#m   B/D#   E   A E   B/D#
My soul is longing for the Spirit of God to come

Bridge
A2   Bsus4
Spirit of God, breathe upon us
G#m   A
We are here for You, so fill us up again
C#m B/D# E E/G# A E   B
                          So fill us up again
C#m B/D# E E/G# A E B

Nick Drake and Becky Drake
© 2022 Integrity Music Europe (Admin by Integrity Music ltd)

CCLI #: 7198863

Further resources for this song are available at
ccli.com/songbook

OH WHAT A DAY   9

Nick Drake and Becky Drake
Suggested Key: E
BPM: 82 (4/4)

Verse 1
```
E          A           B
It was the day that history had longed for
E          A         B
It was the day that split time in two
E              A         B
And as the star hung over the stable
      A      B    E
It shone for Emmanuel
```

Verse 2
```
It was the day when Shepherds went searching,
It was the day when wise men bowed down,
All eyes were fixed on Jesus the baby
His name was Emmanuel
```

Chorus
```
         B               C#m
Oh what a day, when Jesus came
     A              B
God with us in our darkness,
         B            C#m
Oh what a day, glorious day,
     A             B
God came into our world
         E
Oh what a day!
```

Verse 3
It was the day, that God sent a Saviour,
It was the start, of His master plan,
And as the angels shone round the manger
They sang for Emmanuel

Verse 4
```
C#m            A             B
We sing today, because of Lord Jesus
C#m           A         B
We gather here because He was born
F#m           A            B
We celebrate the start of God's victory,
       A      B    E
It began with Emmanuel
```

Nick Drake and Becky Drake
© 2007 Song Solutions Daybreak (Admin. by Song Solutions www.songsolutions.org)

CCLI #: 5100165

Further resources for this song are available at
ccli.com/songbook

10 THIS IS THE KINGDOM

Sam Blake and Ian Yates
Suggested Key: A
BPM: 96 (4/4)

Verse 1

```
A        D    G       (G#)
  Everyone is welcome
A        D    G       (G#)
  Everyone is seen
A        D    G       (G#)
  No one is forgotten,
A        D    G       (G#)
  Everyone is free
```

Chorus

```
          A     D     G
This is the kingdom, The kingdom of God
                       A     D     G
We're seeking the kingdom, The kingdom of God
         A                D
What's down is up, What's up is down
         G                    D/F#
The ways of the world are flipped around
              A     D     G
In the kingdom,  The kingdom of God
```

Verse 2

We will stand together (standing in Your love)
We will trust our King (no doubt, no fear)
We will serve like Jesus (He's our hero)
Give Him everything

Bridge

```
F         G           Am
  There's a place where the lost are found
F         G           Am
  There's a place where the last are first
F         G           Am
  There's a place where the weak are strong
            F    E   (E/G#)
  Where we belong
```

End (Tag)

```
A                    C           D
We are living in the kingdom of our God
              F              G
(it's upside down) (the lost are found)
A                    C           D
We are living in the kingdom of our God
              F              G
(it's upside down) (the last are first)
A                    C           D
We are living in the kingdom of our God
              F              G
(it's upside down) (The weak are strong)
A                    C           D
We are living in the kingdom of our God
              F           G
(it's upside down)
```

Sam Blake and Ian Yates
© 2023 Song Solutions Daybreak (Admin. by Song Solutions www.songsolutions.org)

CCLI #: 7213705

Outstanding.
I don't know what we'd do without you!

- UK church customer, CCLI Customer Survey, 2022.

COPYRIGHT MADE EASY

As churches harness technology and a wealth of creative content, the issues around copyright can be confusing. CCLI's licences provide a simple, comprehensive, and affordable copyright solution.

CCLI® Connected solutions for your worship

Find out more at **ccli.com/family**

CCLI Christian Copyright Licensing International. Registered in England & Wales: 2580472
Unit 16-17, Pacific House, 1 Easter Island Place, Eastbourne BN23 6FA, UK.